The Heart of Old Edinburgh

by

Margeorie Mekie

The "YOUNGER" Generation

Wm YOUNGER & Co's Scotch Ale

BREWED IN EDINBURGH.

One of the many postcards that were published to advertise Younger's ales.

FURTHER READING

The books listed below were used by the author during her research. None of them are available from Stenlake Publishing. Those interested in finding out more are advised to contact their local bookshop or reference library.

'Aye Ready', The History of the Edinburgh Fire Brigade, A. Reid, 1974
Collins Encyclopaedia of Scotland, J. & J. Keay (ed.), 1994
Edinburgh and the Lothians, Theo Lang, 1952
Moray Park Maltings, William Younger & Co. Ltd.
Old and New Edinburgh, James Grant, 1880
Ordnance Gazetteer of Scotland, 1882
Picturesque Edinburgh, Katharine F. Lockie, 1899
Romantic Edinburgh, John Geddie, 1900
Through Memory's Window, Edinburgh 1860–1927, D. A. Small
Traditions of Edinburgh, Robert Chambers, 1824
Edinburgh Post Office Directories

ACKNOWLEDGEMENTS

I would like to thank Jim Brown, Gareth Burgess and Robin Sherman who kindly lent postcards from their collections. The staff of the Edinburgh Room of Edinburgh Central Library for their assistance with my research. Sybil Innes for sharing her knowledge of the history of the Edinburgh Floral Clock. Peter Williamson for his knowledge of the Maudslay bus. Fiona Gebbie for allowing me access to her copy of Picturesque Edinburgh. The many members of the Lothian Postcard Club, who not only gave their support but many of whom very kindly offered relevant postcards. Oliver van Helden for his wise counsel in the selection of pictures and cards. In conclusion this book would not have been possible without the help from my husband David, who has shown great tolerance and patience, as well as giving practical help with the proof reading.

© Margeorie Mekie 2004
First published in the united Kingdom, 2004, by Stenlake Publishing Ltd.
Telephone: 01290 551122
Printed by Cordfall Ltd., Glasgow, G21 2QA

ISBN 1 84033 302 2

The publishers regret that they cannot supply copies of any pictures featured in this book.

WHITEHORSE CLOSE – EDINBURGH

J. D. S. & C°. 31

INTRODUCTION

Edinburgh's earliest history centres around its castle, perched high on an outcrop of volcanic rock overlooking Princes Street. The old city was built on a sloping ridge stretching down from the castle to the Palace of Holyrood, and the street connecting the two is called the Royal Mile. It is divided into five principal sections: Castlehill, Lawnmarket, High Street, Canongate and the Abbey Strand. Leading off this main thoroughfare, between tenements up to twelve storeys high, were hundreds of very steep and narrow alleys known as closes and wynds. A wynd was a lane or small street which acted as a thoroughfare, while a close led to houses or shops and was locked at night.

The Royal Mile and the streets either side of it comprise Edinburgh's Old Town, the most ancient part of the city. Princes Street and the Georgian development to its north make up what is known as the New Town. This book focuses principally on the Old Town, but includes Princes Street and its gardens, which are overlooked by the historic Royal Mile. These areas form the nucleus – or 'heart' – of old Edinburgh.

During the eighteenth and nineteenth centuries Scotland's capital city was overpopulated, with the closes and wynds of the Old Town acting as a particular focus of overcrowding. Sometimes up to 1,000 people lived in a single close. Many of these cramped alleyways were named after a landlord or important resident, while others reflected the activity carried out there, such as Fishmarket Close, Fleshmarket Close, Bakehouse Close, Stamp Office Close and Playhouse Close. Although many respectable people lived in the closes, there were also those who consumed large quantities of alcohol while their starving children could be found begging or stealing. Many of the children who attended the city's Ragged School were the offspring of drunkards.

At ten o'clock at night a drum could be heard in the vicinity of the Royal Mile, the signal for the windows of the tenements to be thrown open. With a loud cry of 'gardyloo' (watch out below), occupants threw dirty water and refuse which had accumulated during the day out of the windows of the houses and into the streets below. Woe betide anyone caught underneath this deluge of filth! Partly as a result of this practice, many of the closes were stinking, dirty places, with pigs and dogs running about freely. Sanitation was poor and disease was rife. In an analysis of observation we have to make is that a number of the tenements are altogether unfit to be habited by men. The walls of them are ruinous and the internal parts are decayed. Despite this, however, they are crammed full of people. There is not a drop of water in the Wynd that we have been able to discover and all water must be carried from the well in the adjoining close. There is no drain in the Wynd and consequently all the filth of the place remains on the surface.'

To the north of the castle lay the Nor' Loch, filling the hollow now occupied by Princes Street Gardens. Heretics and suspected witches were doused in the waters of the loch (which was also a convenient dumping ground for rubbish from the Old Town) before being strangled on Castlehill. Despite this, it became a centre for recreation with boating in the summer and skating in the winter. In 1763 part of the loch was drained and plans were drawn up to bridge the valley by constructing an earthen mound connecting the Old Town to the fields in the north that were soon to be developed as the Georgian New Town, at the time the biggest city development in the world. One of the new thoroughfares to be laid out was Princes Street, whose south-facing facades overlook the well-maintained Princes Street Gardens, with the castle in the background adjoined by the elegant houses on the brow of the Castlehill.

Most of the images in this book are reproduced from postcards and date from the heyday of their production in the early years of the twentieth century. They illustrate many aspects of the Old Town of Edinburgh, showing some features that have remained constant over the past 150 years, and many that have changed.

THE GRASSMARKET

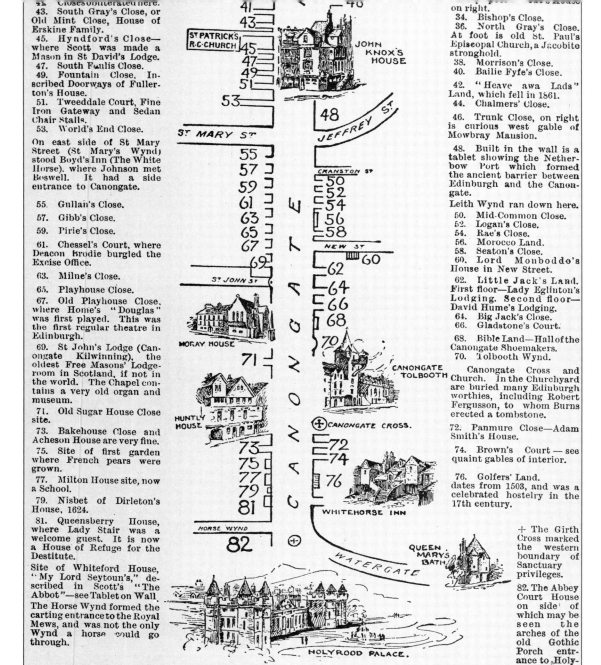

41. Closes obliterated here.

43. South Gray's Close, or Old Mint Close, House of Erskine Family.

45. Hyndford's Close—where Scott was made a Mason in St David's Lodge.

47. South Foulis Close.

49. Fountain Close, Inscribed Doorways of Fullerton's House.

51. Tweeddale Court, Fine Iron Gateway and Sedan Chair Stalls.

53. World's End Close.

On east side of St Mary Street (St Mary's Wynd) stood Boyd's Inn (The White Horse), where Johnson met Boswell. It had a side entrance to Canongate.

55. Gullan's Close.

57. Gibb's Close.

59. Pirie's Close.

61. Chessel's Court, where Deacon Brodie burgled the Excise Office.

63. Milne's Close.

65. Playhouse Close.

67. Old Playhouse Close, where Home's "Douglas" was first played. This was the first regular theatre in Edinburgh.

69. St John's Lodge (Canongate Kilwinning), the oldest Free Masons' Lodgeroom in Scotland, if not in the world. The Chapel contains a very old organ and museum.

71. Old Sugar House Close site.

73. Bakehouse Close and Acheson House are very fine.

75. Site of first garden where French pears were grown.

77. Milton House site, now a School.

79. Nisbet of Dirleton's House, 1624.

81. Queensberry House, where Lady Stair was a welcome guest. It is now a House of Refuge for the Destitute.

Site of Whiteford House, "My Lord Seytoun's," described in Scott's "The Abbot"—see Tablet on Wall.

The Horse Wynd formed the carting entrance to the Royal Mews, and was not the only Wynd a horse could go through.

34. Bishop's Close.

36. North Gray's Close. At foot is old St. Paul's Episcopal Church, a Jacobite stronghold.

38. Morrison's Close.

40. Bailie Fyfe's Close.

42. "Heave awa Lads" Land, which fell in 1861.

44. Chalmers' Close.

46. Trunk Close, on right is curious west gable of Mowbray Mansion.

48. Built in the wall is a tablet showing the Netherbow Port which formed the ancient barrier between Edinburgh and the Canongate.

Leith Wynd ran down here.

50. Mid-Common Close.

52. Logan's Close.

54. Rae's Close.

56. Morocco Land.

58. Seaton's Close.

60. Lord Monboddo's House in New Street.

62. Little Jack's Land. First floor—Lady Eglinton's Lodging. Second floor—David Hume's Lodging.

64. Big Jack's Close.

66. Gladstone's Court.

68. Bible Land—Hall of the Canongate Shoemakers.

70. Tolbooth Wynd.

Canongate Cross and Church. In the Churchyard are buried many Edinburgh worthies, including Robert Fergusson, to whom Burns erected a tombstone.

72. Panmure Close—Adam Smith's House.

74. Brown's Court — see quaint gables of interior.

76. Golfers' Land. dates from 1503, and was a celebrated hostelry in the 17th century.

✝ The Girth Cross marked the western boundary of Sanctuary privileges.

82. The Abbey Court House on side of which may be seen the arches of the old Gothic Porch entrance to Holyrood.

* Wynd signifies a lane which winds from street to street. These were open day and night. Closes on the other hand were usually entrances to patrician dwellings, and were closed at night.

This Edwardian map of the Royal Mile shows many of the places of interest along its length, plus several of the closes and wynds.

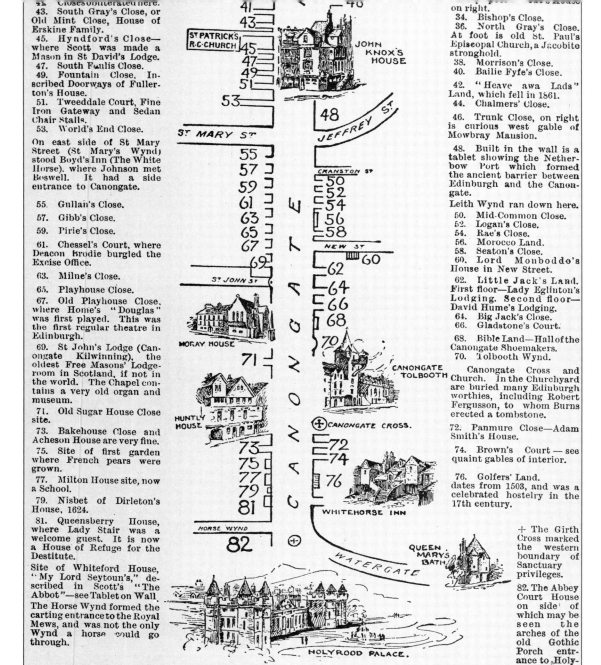

The Royal Historic Mile of Edinburgh.

In the Castle are the Crown and Jewels of James V. and Queen Mary, The Parliament Hall, Queen Margaret's Chapel, etc.

1. Cannon Ball House (at back see stone runnels for shutters, dating from days before the use of glass).

2. Allan Ramsay's House on Castle Hill, now part of Ramsay Gardens. In front is Reservoir for first Water Supply 1680-1, which is still in use.

3. Doorway of Gordon House, seen from Boswell's Court.

* Outlook Tower (see advertisement on back.)

4. Semple Doorways with Inscriptions.

5. Bailie Macmorran's House, Riddle's Close.

6. Milne's Court, the first Square in Edinburgh.

7. Brodie's Court and Roman Eagle Hall — Fine ceiling, 1645-6.

8. James' Court, where Boswell received Dr Johnson. Hume, Blair, and other celebrities lived here.

9. Buchanan's Court

To Greyfriars Churchyard, Museum, and University.

10. Lady Stair's House, restored & gifted by Lord Rosebery to the City. Burns' first Lodging was opposite the old doorway.

11. New County Buildings.

13. Advocates', Signet and Solicitors' Libraries.

Heart of Midlothian.

12. Wardrop's Court.

15. Parliament Hall and Courts of Justice. John Knox's Grave.

14. Byers' Close and Commendator Adam Bothwell's House, seen from Advocates' Close, described in Scott's "Guy Mannering" and Stevenson's "Catriona."

17. City Mercat Cross, restored by W. E. Gladstone.

19. Police Chambers and Lost Property Offices. Scene of great fire in 1824.

16. Warriston's Close, Royal Exchange, now Municipal Buildings, contains a fine Museum of Edinburgh antiquities (open to visitors).

21. Old Fishmarket Close where George Heriot resided.

23. Borthwick's Close.

25. Old Assembly Close.

27. Burnet's Close.

29. Bell's Wynd.

18. Allen's Close, at foot of which Deacon Brodie "planked" his burglar's tools.

31. Scottish Children's League of Pity, S.P.C.C., and Children's Shelter.

33. Stevenlaw's Close.

20. Craig's Close.

22. Old Post Office Close.

Leading to the Cowgate or "South Gait"—once the fashionable quarter of Edinburgh.

24. Anchor Close, where Andro Hart's and W. Smellie's Printing Offices were, and where the Cape Club met.

To Old University and Southern Suburbs.

26. Old Stamp Office Close

28. Lyon's Close.

30. Fleshmarket Close.

* Site of Darien Co.'s Offices.

Once a Wynd.

35. Dickson's Close.

37. Cant's Close.

39. Strichen's Close and Abbot of Melrose's Lodging.

32. Carrubber's Close

The view from the castle looking over the eastern part of the city. To the right is the domed Bank of Scotland building, with the gardens and paths of Princes Street Gardens in the foreground, along with the opening of the tunnel which takes trains under the Mound to Waverley station. (The Mound is the wide, curving street that connects Princes Street to the High Street.) The Scott Monument is prominent in Princes Street Gardens, and the old Calton Prison is in the centre background.

Situated high on a rocky outcrop, Edinburgh Castle commands a powerful position over the city. Details of its early history are unclear, but it has been a stronghold for well over 1,000 years. Many romantic events have taken place within its walls, and it has been besieged and captured several times. Today one enters the castle over a ditch which at one time would have been controlled by a drawbridge, continuing up the hill past the governor's house and barracks to reach the site of the original castle. The main buildings are in the castle yard – the fifteenth century palace, the great hall (still in use today for important occasions), and the newest building, the Scottish National War Memorial. The elaborate Ross Fountain (foreground) in Princes Street Gardens was gifted by local citizen Daniel Ross and erected in 1869. Dean Ramsay described the fountain as 'Grossly indecent and disgusting; insulting and offensive to the moral feelings of the community and disgraceful to the city'! Despite these harsh comments it remains an accepted landmark today.

208853 J.V. Changing the Guard, Edinburgh Castle

Created in 1753, the castle Esplanade was originally used as a parade ground, and in times past witches and martyrs were executed here. Several monuments have been erected on the Esplanade in memory of Scottish soldiers, and it is also the site of the Military Tattoo held annually during the Edinburgh International Festival. This begins with massed military bands marching across the drawbridge and out of the castle, and continues with a varied programme of entertainment provided by participants from all over the world. The culmination of the tattoo – enjoyed live by over 217,000 people during its three-week programme – is an impressive firework display. The niches either side of the entrance gateway to the castle contain bronze statues of Wallace and Bruce which were unveiled in 1929 on the 600th anniversary of the granting of King Robert the Bruce's charter to Edinburgh. After passing through the massive gateway and guard house, visitors to the castle continue up the narrow cobbled path to the ancient portcullis gate. The building over its archway, visible at the right-hand edge of this picture, is known as the Argyll Tower and was once used as a prison. Several illustrious men, including one of the Earls of Argyll, have been imprisoned here. Although this postcard is titled 'Changing the Guard', there would appear to be armoured cars to the right of the Esplanade and the large phalanx of soldiers marching out of the castle suggests a more significant event.

8

The King of Uganda being given a conducted tour of the castle during a visit to Edinburgh, possibly in 1908. Many attackers have been forced to retire after coming under a hail of cannon fire from the massive portholes of the half-moon battery, 510 feet above sea level. The ancient Mons Meg, an enormous cannon which has been used to protect the castle many times in the past, is kept nearby. Its origins are unclear. Some authorities say it was forged at Mons in Belgium in 1476, while others maintain it was made by a Scottish blacksmith from Galloway. Adjacent to the half-moon battery is the Edinburgh time gun, which is fired every day at one o'clock and can be heard for several miles. A 21-gun salute is fired from this battery on royal and state occasions.

The castle battery commands fine views over the city, and on a clear day visitors can see across the Firth of Forth to Fife. West Princes Street Gardens are in the foreground of this view, with the shops of Princes Street in the background. Just out of sight is the Ross Bandstand, gifted by William Ross in 1935. Bands play frequently throughout the summer for the pleasure of locals and tourists. When the Nor' Loch was drained to make way for Princes Street Gardens many skeletons were found in it!

10

"H.R.H. The Prince of Wales Unveiling Scottish War Memorial Edinburgh Castle July 1927"

The Scottish National War Memorial is the most recent of the castle's buildings. Constructed in 1927 on the site's most elevated point, it is an elaborate shrine that commands an atmosphere of subdued silence. Within the pages of the books of remembrance that are on display are rolls of honour naming thousands of men and women who died fighting for their country as members of Scottish regiments. The hall of honour is bedecked with flags of many nations and contains beautiful stained glass windows.

11

At the east end of the castle Esplanade, where Castlehill commences, is an early seventeenth century building known as Cannonball House. Embedded in its west gable is a cannon ball, thought by many to have been fired from the half-moon battery during the castle's blockade of 1745. However, the Castlehill Reservoir was supplied with water from Comiston Springs and a more logical explanation is that the cannon ball marked the gravitation height of the water supply, which was first piped to this area in 1681.

12

D 915

The Lawnmarket is situated between Castlehill and the High Street, and may have acquired its name from the 'lawn merchants' whose stalls and booths were laid out with webs of cloth. On this short stretch of the Royal Mile there are many entrances to narrow closes including Buchanan's Court, Brodie's Close and Riddle's Court (on the south side), with Lady Stair's Close, James' Court and Milne's Court to the north. Gladstone's Land, with its arcaded front, is on the left in this picture. It was originally the property of Thomas Gledstanes, a merchant and burgess, and is now owned by the National Trust for Scotland, which has furnished it to represent the home of a well-to-do family of the late seventeenth century. The beautiful painted beams and mural decorations date from that period. The sign in the foreground indicates the entrance to Lady Stair's House Museum, while the Robert Burns Tavern advertises McEwan's ales.

13

Lady Stair's Close takes its name from Elizabeth, Dowager Countess of Stair, a notable leader of fashion in her day. The close is entered from the Lawnmarket, where a tablet over the entrance states 'In a house on the east side of this close Robert Burns lived during his first visit to Edinburgh, 1786'. Having ventured through the narrow opening, the close opens out to a large courtyard where the seventeenth century Lady Stair's House is situated. In 1907 the 5th Earl of Rosebery presented the house to the Town Council of Edinburgh for use as a museum. Many literary artefacts can be seen here, notably relating to Robert Burns, Sir Walter Scott and Robert Louis Stevenson.

Brodie's Close, Edinburgh.

William Brodie, after whom this close is named, had a reputation for being a prosperous and pious citizen until his daring robbery of the city's excise office in 1788. He was Deacon of the Wrights and Masons of Edinburgh, but had a taste for betting, becoming a frequenter of a low gambling house in Fleshmarket Close but managing to still remain a highly respected member of the town council. In 1787 a series of robberies were committed, with houses and shops entered and valuables stolen. It was during the robbery of one house that a panic-stricken lady thought that her assailant was Deacon Brodie. However, as the idea seemed so utterly ridiculous she remained silent. On the night of 5 March, Brodie, dressed all in black, forced entry into the excise office in Chessel's Court with two accomplices. During a previous visit he had taken an impression of the key to the cashier's room. At half past eight, the deputy solicitor returned to the office unexpectedly. Without creating suspicion Brodie walked quickly past him, and the rogues got clear away, but with the unexpectedly small amount of £16. His two accomplices hurried to the New Town, while Brodie changed his attire and proceeded to visit his mistress, Jean Watt, in Liberton's Wynd. Edinburgh was in turmoil as the rumours spread. Rewards were offered and one of Brodie's accomplices, Humphrey Moore, who was already under sentence of transportation, resolved to turn King's evidence. Brodie was charged and sentenced to be hanged, mounting the scaffold at the west end of the tolbooth wearing a black suit, his hair dressed and powdered. As the bells of St Giles Cathedral tolled he died – having neither confessed nor denied his guilt – in front of a vast crowd of spectators who had come to witness his execution.

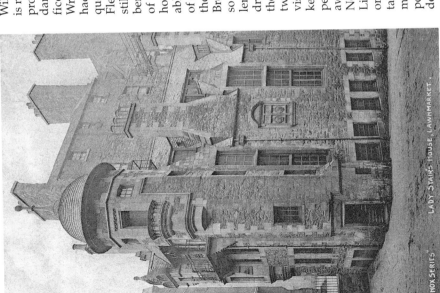

KNOX SERIES

LADY STAIR'S HOUSE, LAWNMARKET.

Edinburgh firemen pose for a photograph outside Warriston Close. James Braidwood was the city's firemaster from 1824 to 1832, and preferred to select recruits for his brigade from the ranks of Edinburgh's slaters, masons, plumbers, carpenters and smiths. Here the men look very smart in their uniforms of white canvas trousers, black jackets with brass buttons, and leather belts with brass buckles, to which were attached axes, hose couplings, spanners and a length of cord. There were four companies, each under the command of a captain or sergeant, and distinguished by the colours of their helmets (red, blue, yellow and grey). James Braidwood resigned his Edinburgh post to become superintendent of the London Fire Engine Establishment.

Set into the pavement to the west of St Giles Cathedral is the outline of a heart marking the spot where, until the beginning of the nineteenth century, Edinburgh's old tolbooth stood. The tolbooth was built of polished ashlar and was five storeys in height. At its west end was a projection which served as a scaffold for executions. On the top of its pointed gable was an iron spike on which the heads of criminals were stuck after execution. It was used as a prison after 1640, and the superstitious still sometimes express their feelings for its penal functions by spitting on the heart! The phrase 'Heart of Midlothian' is derived from the title of the novel by Sir Walter Scott which featured the tolbooth's jail.

—Proclamation of King George V
Mercat Cross, Edinburgh, 10th May.

It is believed that St Giles Cathedral was erected on or near the spot where the city's original parish church stood, an early predecessor of which is thought to have been founded *circa* AD 1120. The fabric of the present cathedral has been altered and restored on many occasions. There are memorials within it to famous Scottish churchmen, statesmen, philanthropists and soldiers, including tributes to those men of the Royal Scots who were killed in the First World War. The spire, or 'crown of St Giles', is a representation of an imperial crown and can be seen from most parts of the city. In 1560, when still called the parish church, John Knox was minister here. There were no pews and instead people brought along chairs and stools of their own, listening to Knox with great intent while he preached. On Sunday 23 July 1637 Charles I ordered that the English church service be read in every parish church in Scotland. Dean Hannay was the officiating minister that day, and as he began his sermon a kail-wife (cabbage seller) by the name of Jenny Geddes is said to have flung her stool at him, striking him on the head. The space south of St Giles was formerly a graveyard and is now known as Parliament Square.

The Mercat Cross is situated immediately to the east of St Giles Cathedral and was once the focus of not only civic, but also national affairs in the city. Merchants, noblemen and ministers were among those who crowded round this handsome octagonal building, with its tall central pillar surmounted by a unicorn, to hear state and royal proclamations. The original cross, dating back to the time of David I, was rebuilt in 1617, then demolished in 1756. In 1885 it was reconstructed, based on the likely design of the 1617 restoration.

16

There are seven arches fronting the City Chambers, built in 1753–61 to designs by John Adam and originally called the Royal Exchange. The Stone of Remembrance is situated beneath the middle arch, while underneath the chambers is a warren of ancient closes. One of these is Mary King's Close, which is open to the public, although not suitable for the claustrophobic or faint of heart. Indeed, it is a place of terror to the superstitious. Mary King is believed to have been the daughter of the close's owner, Alexander King, and in 1645 an outbreak of the plague started there with practically every inhabitant perishing. Mary, who was a Catholic, was blamed by the Protestants for the outbreak, and all the houses were boarded up with the close eventually being shut. For many generations its houses remained unused, and it gradually became a place of mystery and horror. Prior to the building of the Royal Exchange, Mary King's Close was roofless and the ruined buildings flourished with weeds, wallflowers, grass and even small trees. It has since been restored, and today guided tours take visitors back in time, gingerly leading them down the stairs to the entrance of the close and on inside, where the tiny bakehouse, long, low-ceilinged tavern, and slaughterhouse can all be seen. It is an eerie experience, and many people state that they definitely feel a presence.

Looking up High Street towards the Lawnmarket, where the Tron Kirk stands at the corner of South Bridge in Hunter Square. The church took its name from its location opposite the public weighing beam, called the Salt-Tron. In 1824, during a great fire which devastated the south side of the High Street from the Tron to St Giles, it lost the upper part of its original steeple, a lead-covered wooden affair, but acquired a handsome new spire in 1828. While the right-hand side of the street as seen in this view remains much the same today, a stylish new hotel, whose architecture is very much in keeping with that of the old town, has replaced the greater part of the tenements on the left, which were demolished along with Dickson's, Cant's and Strichen's Closes.

18

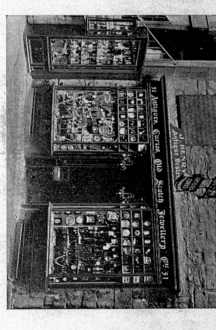
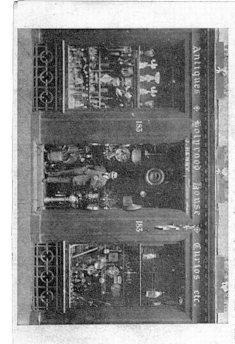

'HEAVE AWA' LADS' MEMORIAL, HIGH STREET.

At midnight on 24 November 1861 a thunderous crash was heard at 107 High Street. After standing for some 250 years, the stately tenement at the head of Bailie Fyfe's Close collapsed without warning, killing 35 people. While digging through the rubble looking for the dead and wounded, rescuers heard a young lad (Joseph McIvor) call out 'Heave awa', lads, I'm no deid yet'. He survived, and when the tenement was rebuilt the following year a likeness was carved above the entrance to the adjacent Paisley Close at 101 High Street, with a scroll bearing the slightly anglicised wording 'Heave awa' chaps, I'm no dead yet'.

John Henry had antique and jewellery shops at 51, 53, 85, 87 and 183 High Street, specialising in Old Sheffield Plate, china, antique English and French furniture and fine jewels. The shop at No. 51 was formerly known as Moubray House. It is an ancient relic of Edinburgh and probably the oldest house in the Old Town. Situated next to John Knox's House, it looks similar today, although the jewellery in the window has been replaced by shoes. In the early eighteenth century Daniel Defoe edited the *Edinburgh Courant* from Moubray House.

19

The quaint building in the centre of this picture with its stone staircase descending to the pavement is called John Knox's House. It has been suggested that Knox died here on 24 November 1572, and the building contains a museum featuring artefacts relating to him. However, it is possible that John Knox actually lived nearer to the scene of his ministrations in St Giles Cathedral, and in 1572 the house may have been occupied by a goldsmith, James Mossman, who could at one time have owned the adjacent shop called Moubray House. Near John Knox's House brass bricks are set in the roadway to mark the site of the Netherbow Port. This gateway separated the city proper from: the Burgh of the Canongate and was the principal route in and out of the Old Town. It was built in 1513 and survived for approximately 250 years before being demolished to widen the roadway down to Holyrood Palace. The building incorporated a tower with spires, plus spikes where the heads of criminals were placed. It formed part of Edinburgh's defensive city wall, named the Flodden Wall after the disaster of Flodden. A portion of the wall remains today at the bottom of St Mary's Street heading up towards the Pleasance.

20

The effigy of a Moor wearing a turban and a necklace of beads adorns the building known as Morocco Land. Various stories have been proposed regarding the identity of the figure, who may have been Andrew Gray, an Edinburgh man who left the city in 1635 to avoid being arrested for rioting, and returned ten years later as the captain of a Barbary vessel. Seeking revenge against Lord Provost John Smith, he ended up curing the provost's daughter of the plague and marrying her. An alternative tale tells of an Edinburgh woman on a voyage being kidnapped and sold to the Emperor of Morocco, after which she became a favourite in his harem. Her letters home are said to have led to her brother conducting commercial transactions with Morocco, making him a small fortune, out of which he built this stately mansion in the Canongate. It has also been suggested that the figure of the Moor is simply a trader's sign! Next door to P. S. Smith the baker, at No. 279, is the entrance to the tenement flats above the shops, while No. 281 is Reid's Close. Note the washing hanging out to dry on poles.

Despite being one of a long line of illustrious golfers, John Paterson was nonetheless an impoverished shoemaker. Having partnered the Duke of York (later James VII) against two English noblemen at a game of golf on Leith Links c.1671, and being crowned victor, he built this stylish six-storey gabled mansion in the Canongate, on top of which he placed the Paterson coat of arms with their motto 'Far and Sure'. A slab above the entrance carried an inscription in Latin, the last line (in English), stating 'I Hate No Person', an anagram of John Paterson. Having been won by the gambling tendencies of its owner, it is thought that Golfer's Land may have later been lost as a result of his love for high stakes. It has now been demolished.

21

The present tolbooth is situated in the Canongate opposite Huntly House, and was erected in 1591 on the same spot as its predecessor. It was where tolls and taxes were collected, and included a tiny, overcrowded prison which housed debtors until the Calton Prison was built in 1840. At that point the former jail became a registrar's office. The ground floor of the tolbooth latterly housed a fire station, police office, court and council chambers, and the fire station entrance can be seen on the right in this picture. The building's most prominent feature is its clock, which is dated 1884 and reached by a sixteenth century turnpike stair. Today the tolbooth houses an exhibition called 'The People's Story' where visitors can gain an insight into Edinburgh life as it once was.

Today Whitehorse Close is a quaint backwater, with its houses attractively painted and the courtyard adorned with flowers and shrubs, although in the 1880s it was very dilapidated and decayed. Towards the back of the close is an outside stair leading to the Whitehorse Inn, after which the well-known brand of whisky was named. The close is situated at the bottom of the Canongate and in 1749 was the departure point for the first coach between Edinburgh and London.

WHITE HORSE CLOSE, EDINBURGH.

01065

BACK OF WHITEHORSE CLOSE, CANONGATE, EDINBURGH.

The Moray Park Maltings were owned by William Younger & Co. and were located in Marionville Road off London Road. At harvest-time there was a steady stream of lorries conveying barley not only to Moray Park but also Younger's other large maltings at Canonmills. On arrival the bags of barley were emptied into elevators and conveyed to the drying plant. Eventually the malt would be sent to the Abbey and Holyrood Brewhouses, with brown ale and stout made from the dark malt and pale ale from its lighter counterpart. Moray Park also had large cellars for the storage of casks of beer, as well as an extensive cooperage.

The present Palace of Holyroodhouse, nestling at the foot of Arthur's Seat, was built for King Charles II between 1671–8. To its north-east are the ruined remains of Holyrood Abbey, constructed in 1128 by David 1, King of the Scots. A portrait gallery in the palace displays paintings said to depict over 100 Scottish monarchs. Many romantic and historical tales are associated with Holyrood, and in particular Queen Mary's bedroom. Her bed was richly hung with crimson damask, green fringes and tassels. Half concealed behind a tapestry is a small door leading to the Queen's secret stair. She used this daily when going to and from prayers in the kirk, and it was by this route that the assassins of Rizzio entered the royal apartments in 1566. Scottish noblemen were so jealous of the influence of the Italian Rizzio, who was Secretary to the Queen, that one evening he was

assassinated in her presence. His body was dragged out of the room and the bloodstains on the floor are said to be still visible. Rizzio was an accomplished musician and often played to Queen Mary:

She thought of all her blighted hopes – the dreams of youth's brief day,
And summoned Rizzio with his lute, and bade the minstrel play.
The songs she loved in early years – the songs of gay Navarre
The songs perchance that erst were sung by gallant Chatelar.

The palace is the official residence of the royal family when its members visit Edinburgh, but is open to the public when they are not staying there.

Calton Hill Prison & Royal High School, Edinburgh.

The substantial building in the centre of this picture is the former Calton Prison (seen from the rear), with the Royal High School to its right. By the end of the nineteenth century this was the most important school in Scotland, and its roll of former scholars includes many distinguished members of the professions, as well as men of literature, science and politics. The Nelson Monument and the National Monument can be seen in the background crowning Calton Hill. The former is 100 feet high and was built to commemorate the deeds of Viscount Horatio Nelson, who was killed in action aboard his ship *Victory* at Trafalgar in 1805. The uncompleted National Monument, a model of the Parthenon in Athens, occupies a prominent position on the hilltop. It was designed to commemorate the achievements of Scottish officers and soldiers who fell in the Napoleonic Wars, but a lack of funding meant that in 1830, four years after construction began, the project was abandoned. There is also an observatory on the hill, which was built in 1776 with extensions in a Greek design added in 1818.

26

Calton Prison, long since demolished, stood on the lower slopes of the Calton Hill occupying the brow of a cliff overhanging the back of the Canongate. It was built on the site of the batteries used against the forces of Queen Mary's party in 1571. Three groups of buildings were erected at different dates within different enclosures for separate purposes. The governor's house was surmounted by a round, castellated tower and perched on the edge of a precipice overlooking the old town. In the background of this picture is the castle, with Princes Street leading westwards to the right.

The firm of William McKinnell, tobacco and snuff manufacturers, was situated in Picardy Place. The company advertised that its famed tobaccos were smoked in preference to all others, both at home and abroad by the British and Colonial troops, to whom thousands of tons were supplied. The reverse of this advertising postcard reads:

Domestic Happiness is secured by using
McKinnell's Tobaccos.
No Ruffled Tempers
No Burned Tongues.

This picture shows McKinnell's premises decorated for the visit of King Edward VII to Edinburgh in May 1903.

Andrew Jupp opened his first shop as a 'musical seller' in 1862/3 at 4 Ronaldson Buildings, and shortly afterwards moved to 95 Kirkgate, Leith. His stay there was short-lived and Edinburgh street directories list his music warehouse as being at 48 Leith Street in Edinburgh (illustrated here) from 1864 until 1916. Mr Jupp died at the age of 83 in August 1915, having survived his wife Amelia by five months.

In 1759 it was decided to build a bridge from High Street northwards to the site where Register House would be constructed a few years later, thus connecting the Old and New Towns. The Nor' Loch was partly drained and the foundation stone of the new bridge laid in 1763 (although building didn't commence until 1765). North Bridge opened in 1772, and two years later magistrates issued a proclamation stating that 'all beggars found in the streets will be imprisoned in the dark vaults beneath the North Bridge and there fed on bread and water'. Faced with the demands of an ever-growing population and resultant increases in traffic, the council constructed a much wider North Bridge in 1894/5. *The Scotsman* newspaper built its impressive offices (right) on the vacant site to the west of the new bridge between its southern end and the High Street. At the time this was the largest building ever erected by private enterprise in Edinburgh. A handsome block, mainly occupied by the department store of Patrick Thomson, was erected on the east side of North Bridge opposite the newspaper offices. Customers spent many enjoyable hours in Patrick Thomson's restaurant, sipping tea and eating scones and cream cakes while listening to the orchestra.

The foundation stone of the new General Post Office building on the site of Shakespeare Square was laid by Prince Albert, the Prince Consort. Designed by Robert Matheson, it was opened to the public in 1866. Before the era of the tramcar, a long wagonette could be seen outside the side door of the post office, waiting to convey the letter carriers with their bundles of letters and newspapers to their 'walks'. Until recently the post office building housed not only public counters but also the Philatelic Bureau. At the time of writing the building is in the process of being demolished, although its frontage is being retained. The statue of the Duke of Wellington on horseback stands outside HM General Register House.

Construction began in 1774 to designs by Robert Adam, but was only fully completed in a second wave of building dating from 1822. Alcoves at the entrance steps were originally for the accommodation of sentries on guard at this government building. These were latterly covered with glass and contained a clock on one side and a barometer on the other. Although the clock remains, the barometer sadly had to be removed as a result of vandalism. 'Old' Register House, recently renamed the National Archives of Scotland, contains the Register of Sasines and Deeds, plus those of the Court of Session, High Court of Justiciary and other courts. New Register House, constructed to its rear from 1859, houses records of births, marriages and deaths, plus census information. Together the buildings are an invaluable resource for those tracing their ancestors.

PRINCES STREET EAST END EDINBURGH.

Taken from the Scott Monument, this picture shows the former North British Hotel (right), whose clocks are always slightly fast, allowing absent-minded travellers an extra minute or two to catch their train! Built in 1902, the five-star hotel is now called the Balmoral. In the foreground are the neatly laid out gardens decorating the roof of the Waverley Market. Entered from Waverley Bridge, this was a large open area where fruit, flowers and vegetables were sold each morning. In the evenings it was used for public meetings and promenade concerts. At Christmas there would be a carnival, while the market halls were also used for trade fairs, exhibitions and circus performances. The former Waverley Market was demolished in 1974.

31

The North British Railway was incorporated in 1844 and opened its line between Edinburgh and Berwick-upon-Tweed – a distance of some 57 miles – in 1846. In those days the approach to Waverley station (above) was by a wooden staircase from Princes Street. Today many commuters travel between Edinburgh and Glasgow via the line which opened between the two cities on 18 February 1842. At that time its terminus was at Haymarket, but in 1847 the railway was extended through Princes Street Gardens to what later became Waverley station (originally called the Joint or General station), and in 1884 additional lines opened to connect the suburbs with the city centre. Inner and outer circle routes enabled speedy access into Edinburgh for commuters from outlying areas.

This Maudslay bus, one of five ordered by the Scottish Motor Traction Company in the early years of the twentieth century, was photographed outside the entrance to Waverley station. It was the second of the batch to come into service, being introduced in early March 1906. Sixteen passengers could sit inside with a further nineteen accommodated on garden-style benches upstairs. Earlier buses were drawn by three horses and in the winter months the vehicles were covered with straw, perhaps to help keep the floor dry. The conductor's steps were at the back and there was a steep staircase leading to the upper deck where passengers sat back to back.

33

In this George Washington Wilson photograph the entrance to the station can be seen on Waverley Bridge. In the background are the antique skyscrapers of Edinburgh's Old Town. The rounded corner of the Cockburn Hotel marks the entrance to Cockburn Street, which was built in 1856 and curves up to the High Street. Advocate's Close is the first of many closes entered from Cockburn Street which connect with the High Street. To the right is the spire of St Giles Cathedral and to the left North Bridge, with Arthur's Seat, one of the seven hills of Edinburgh, in the background. The road curving away to the right leads to the Mound, which crossed the valley of the Nor' Loch.

THE BANK OF SCOTLAND, EDINBURGH.

The head office of the Bank of Scotland (now Halifax Bank of Scotland) is situated on the northern slopes of the Old Town at the top of the Mound, its entrance facing George IV Bridge and its rear overlooking Princes Street. The original building was constructed in 1802–06, but it was renovated and reconstructed between 1864 and 1870 when two additional wings were built. It is Italian in style, originally somewhat plain but now highly ornate, with campanile towers and a great central dome.

Among the many interesting features of Princes Street Gardens are their various monuments. The most prominent and best known is the Scott Monument, built in 1840–46 to the memory of Sir Walter Scott. Four principal arches support a central tower, and 64 statuettes, representing various characters from Scott's literary works, adorn the niches around the monument. A staircase in the interior of the south-west cluster of pillars leads to a small museum which contains an interesting selection of artefacts. For a modest payment visitors may climb the spiral staircase of 287 steps to the top of the monument, where they are rewarded with panoramic views of the city. Under the arches at the base of the monument is a white Carrara marble statue of Sir Walter Scott. He has a plaid over his left shoulder and his favourite deerhound, Maida, at his right foot.

Opposite: The fashionable department store of Jenner's is situated opposite the Scott Monument in Princes Street and was founded in 1838. Its premises were totally destroyed by fire on Saturday 20 November 1892 and the new store, with its imposing elevation, magnificent arcading of doors and windows, and beautiful carvings was opened in May 1895. It was generally believed to be the finest commercial building in Europe. During the 1908 Scottish National Exhibition in Edinburgh, Jenner's could be found at stand No. 141 in the Industrial Hall exhibiting the manufacture of hand-tufted carpets and tartan travelling rugs.

Stand No. 14, Industrial Hall

Working Exhibit showing the Manufacture of Scotch Hand-tufted Carpets and Tartan Travelling Rugs

JENNER'S, EDINBURGH

The most Fashionable Shopping Centre in Scotland

"Jenner's is the shop *par excellence* in Princes Street where high-class goods and moderate prices go together. The name of the firm stands for all that is best in commercial life."

—*Vide Press.*

Jenner's Luncheon and Tea Rooms are the most popular in Edinburgh Pleasantly situated overlooking Princes Street

SCHOOL OF ART & HANOVER STREET

Designed in 1822 by the architect William Playfair, the Royal Scottish Academy stands on Princes Street at the foot of the Mound and is seen here from Hanover Street. Its entrance is approached by a flight of steps leading up to a facade of Grecian-style columns, and the building is surmounted by an enormous statue of Queen Victoria (added in 1844). To the right of the gallery is the Mound, which connects the Old and New Towns. It was gradually formed from earth and rubbish dug out during the building of the foundations of houses in the New Town. For a long time the area was left open, apart from an ungainly wooden staircase, a footpath and a carriageway down the west side. After the erection of the art galleries at the foot of the Mound, the wooden structure was removed and replaced with a broad stone stairway which took the place of the original footpath. A carriage road was built curving round from the Bank of Scotland to Princes Street. At the back of the art gallery beside the stairway is the National Gallery (built 1850–58 and also designed by Playfair), and in the shelter of the two galleries is 'Speaker's Corner', where many people have expressed their opinions on just as many subjects over the years.

38

The world's oldest surviving floral clock is located at the east end of West Princes Street Gardens at the foot of the Mound, and is one of Edinburgh's best-loved attractions. Every year thousands of brightly coloured flowers and shrubs are planted, their design very often marking an important national or international event. The first floral display on this site took place in 1902 when flowers were planted in the shape of a crown in celebration of Edward VII's Coronation. The following year a clock was introduced. The original design only had one hand, the working having come from Elie Parish Church in Fife, but soon afterwards a second hand was added. A cuckoo mechanism was introduced in 1905 and replaced in 1936. The flowers are planted in the spring and removed in October when planning begins for the following year's display. Although obscured, the date at the bottom of this clock reads '1953' with the words 'Elizabeth Regina' round the top honouring the Coronation of Queen Elizabeth that year. Spectators eagerly gather to wait for the cuckoo to pop out of its nest.

A Tribute to the affectionate fidelity of GREYFRIAR'S BOBBY

In 1858 this faithful dog followed the remains of his Master to Greyfriars Churchyard and lingered near the spot until his death in 1872.

With permission erected by the Baroness Burdett Coutts.

GREYFRIARS BOBBY, EDINBURGH. (96)

21592

Mackie's was once the ultimate place to meet with friends for lunch or afternoon tea and sit on the balcony overlooking the beautiful Princes Street Gardens while watching the world go by. A place of fond memories for many of Edinburgh's older residents.

At the top of Candlemaker Row, named after the ancient Incorporation of Candlemakers, is an unusual drinking fountain. It was erected to the memory of a Skye Terrier called Bobby who was faithful to his master, 'Auld Jock' Gray, to the end. After Gray's death in 1858, the dog followed the cortège to Greyfriars' Churchyard where his master was laid to rest. There the animal remained, refusing all attempts to comfort him, and keeping a faithful vigil for years until his own death. The fountain is surmounted by a bronze statue of the terrier, while across the road is Greyfriars' Bobby's Bar. A gravestone was erected to the memory of the dog reading 'Greyfriars' Bobby died 14th January 1872 aged 16 years. Let his loyalty and devotion be a lesson to us all'. This was provided by the Dog Aid Society of Scotland and unveiled on 13 May 1881 by His Royal Highness, the Duke of Gloucester. While this is the most popular interpretation of the Greyfriars' Bobby story, an alternative version tells of a police watchdog owned by one John Gray who showed a similar posthumous loyalty to his master.

40

Originally founded as the Industrial Museum (dating from 1854) and now the Royal Museum of Scotland, the main entrance to this substantial building is in Chambers Street, opposite the statue of Lord Provost William Chambers, Provost of Edinburgh from 1865 to 1869. The foundation stone of the present building (or at least the first section of it to be built) was laid by the Prince Consort in 1861 on his last visit to Edinburgh shortly before his death. The complex has recently been greatly extended. Inside departments cover subjects as diverse as engineering, weaving, printing and natural history. The working models of machinery are some of the finest in the world, and are of great delight to both young and old, who enjoy pressing the buttons and turning the handles.

41

Many famous men and women have passed through the doors of the Grecian-style Surgeons' Hall, and busts and portraits of some of them adorn the walls in the entrance hall and up the stairs. The building's museum is particularly impressive, displaying pathological specimens preserved in large glass jars, including shrunken heads and monstrous babies, one of which has two heads. This is certainly not a place for the squeamish. There are relics associated with the notorious Burke and Hare, the two villains who robbed graveyards, stealing freshly buried bodies and selling them to Dr Robert Knox. When grave-robbing became difficult,

the pair resorted to murder. On more than one occasion Burke and Hare suffocated helpless drunks, leading to their trial and the subsequent hanging of Burke on 28 January 1829. As with their victims, Burke was brought to the anatomist's table and dissected in public.

Doon the close and up the stair
But and ben wi' Burke and Hare.
Burke's the butcher, Hare's the thief
Knox the man that buys the beef.

A patient, accompanied by doctor, nurses and porters, lies on a large wheeled stretcher outside the outpatients department of Edinburgh Royal Infirmary. An early motor ambulance is on hand, while a horse-drawn ambulance wagon is alongside. The city's original infirmary was in the Old Town and dated from 1729. Its successor, in Laurieston Place, was constructed between 1872 and 1879, with many subsequent additions erected partly using money from public subscriptions. The new buildings included pavilions connected to the main hospital by corridors, with separate wards for men and women being the norm. The infirmary dealt with surgical cases, infectious diseases and other medical conditions. Patients were admitted according to the necessity and the urgency of their conditions, and their suitability for hospital treatment.

A SURGICAL WARD.

In the early years of the twentieth century, postcards portraying the exterior of the Royal Infirmary were issued annually, along with interior shots of locations such as the boardroom, ironing room, the nurses' dining room and wards. The postcards could not be written on, as extracts from the hospital's annual report were printed on their reverse. Every year this report showed a deficit, and the postcards begged the public to support this charitable cause according to their means and ability. This card shows a typical ward as it would have appeared within the last 50 years: the shiny waxed floor, patients ensconced in white bed linen, and iron beds complete with wheels for easy manoeuvring are all familiar. In 2003 the Royal Infirmary moved to a brand new building on the southern outskirts of the city.

Turnout, Edinburgh Central Fire Station.

1337

Fire appliances were once manual devices with their pumps worked by muscle power, making them very feeble instruments with which to attack a major conflagration. When horses weren't available, engines were drawn by long ropes pulled by the firemen and anyone else who cared to join in. The Central Fire Station in Laurieston Place replaced an older building in the High Street and was opened on 7 June 1900 by Lord Provost Mitchell, having cost £43,000. A notable feature of the new building was the steel pole by which the firemen housed above could slide down to the engine room when an alarm sounded. The new premises allowed an increase in the strength of the brigade from 41 to 62 men, and the acquisition of ten additional horses. This postcard shows a handsome fire appliance dating from the early years of the twentieth century.

This is the east end of the Grassmarket, where the West Bow follows a steep curve up the hill heading for George IV Bridge with high-storied buildings on either side. Apart from being the site of the old corn market, this was a place of public execution and, in the words of Sir Walter Scott, 'The fatal day was announced to the public by the appearance of a huge black gallows-tree towards the eastern end of the Grassmarket. This ill-omened apparition was of great height, with a scaffold surrounding it, and a double ladder placed against it, for the ascent of the unhappy criminal and the executioner.' The gallows were assembled well before dawn and removed the evening after the execution in the darkness of the night. The last person to be hanged here was James Andrew, who lost his life on 4 February 1784 for the crime of robbery. Today an arrangement of paving stones, in the shape of a cross, is set in the road where the gallows once stood, a grim reminder of days gone by.